JOURNEYS FROM YELLOWSTONE TO THE PAINTED DESERT

RED ROCK YELLOW STONE

PHOTOGRAPHS BY EDWIN FIRMAGE

To John
with best wishes
Ed Firmage
Lake Hotel 7/25/06

COPYRIGHT INFORMATION

Book design, introduction, original haiku & images
© 2005 Edwin J. Firmage. All rights reserved.

Library of Congress Cataloging-in-Publication Data
Firmage, Edwin, 1958 -
Red Rock Yellow Stone:
Journeys from Yellowstone to the Painted Desert /
Edwin Firmage—1st ed.
112 p. 28 x 35 cm.

Summary: A collection of color photographs of National Parks of the western U.S. accompanied by haiku composed by the artist as well as Basho, Buson, Issa, Shiki and others. Includes bibliographic references. Printed on acid-free paper.

ISBN 0-9765693-1-0 (Yellowstone cover)
ISBN 0-9765693-2-9 (Redrock cover)

1. National parks and reserves—West (U.S.)—Pictorial works.
2. Landscape photography—West (U.S.). 3. West (U.S.)—Pictorial works. 4. Nature—Poetry. 5. Haiku—Translations into English.
6. Photography, Artistic. 7. Calligraphy, Japanese. 8. Matsuo, Basho, 1644-1694. 9. Kobayashi, Issa, 1763-1827. 10. Yosano, Buson, 1716-1784. 11. Masaoka, Shiki, 1867-1902.
I.Title II. Firmage, Edwin TR646.U6F57 2005   917.92/59 –dc22

Page 108 constitutes an extension of this page.

www.redrockyellowstone.com

FIRMAGEDITIONS
P. O. Box 9500 • SLC, UT 84109 • 801-424-3041
email: efirmage@firmageditions.com
www.edwinfirmage.com
Book Design: Fairchild Creative & Edwin Firmage

For Reginald Blyth,
Brother Issa, and the rest:
How many mountains!

He who would do good to another must do it in minute particulars.

— WILLIAM BLAKE
Jerusalem

To see the abstract in the concrete and the concrete in the abstract is the essence of art making...

— PAUL RAND
Design Form and Chaos

Use the commonplace to escape the commonplace.

— BUSON

grand canyon, yellowstone

INTRODUCTION: THE ART OF THE ORDINARY

by Edwin Firmage

About the Photographs

Imagining the thoughts of an aging mountain man, Montana novelist A. B. Guthrie wrote:

"As a man got older he felt different about things....He liked rendezvous still, and to see the hills and travel the streams and all, but half the pleasure was in the remembering mind. A place didn't stand alone after a man had been there once. It stood along with the times he had had, with the thoughts he had thought, with the men he had played and fought and drunk with, so when he got there again he was always asking whatever became of so-and-so, asking if the others minded a certain time. It stood with the young him and the former feelings. A river wasn't the same once a man had camped by it. The tree he saw wasn't the same tree if he had only so much as pissed against it. There was the first time and the place alone, and afterwards there was the place and time and the man he used to be, all mixed up, one with the other."*

Landscapes impress themselves on all of us this way. So do other things. Indeed, this merging of things with our thoughts about them — conceptual blending as it's called — is what thought is all about. Until I've seen a door or a tree, the words "door" and "tree" are just meaningless collections of sounds or letters on a page. Once seen, touched, and smelled, however, things merge with the names we give them. These blends in turn combine with one another to create mental webs of association that are the wellspring of the imagination. And, the resulting mix is as unique as each person. No two people see anything identically or react to it in quite the same way.

In a certain sense, then, each of us actively, if unconsciously, creates the world we experience. The world isn't simply something out there that is objectively perceived by a disinterested observer. For example, while a place called Yellowstone exists in its own right, what I know as Yellowstone is the sum of the things I have experienced there. Through my travels in the park and the association of its features with my experiences, I create the entity that is evoked when I hear or read the word Yellowstone. What Yellowstone is independent of me or of the many others who experience it is hard to say, because there is no notion of Yellowstone that is separable from the active and creative involvement of our imagination. We're like the proverbial scientists studying different parts of an elephant, each describing something related but not identical to what others see and feel. The catch is, there is no one with the total view; all views are necessarily partial and colored by individual experience. To see or feel at all is to impose your viewpoint on the world.

But more interesting still is the inverse of the previous notion: Yellowstone creates me. The psychiatrist Carl Jung once observed that the soul is embodied not inside us but in the world we inhabit. What he means is that the I, the self, that seems to stand apart from the world, is given form and identity by the continual interaction of the mind and its environment. The way I think, the symbols, customs, memories, prejudices, and loves that define me are formed in the crucible of my interaction with the

*The Big Sky. Boston: Houghton Mifflin, 2002, 194.

near brigham city, ut

world. In this sense, the world creates me just as I create it. I don't simply think about the things around me; I think with them. They are the building blocks of thought and emotion, and hence of me.

Thus, while it is convenient for me to think of myself symbolically as a thing separate from the world, I am in reality an integral and inseparable part of it. Short-hand language aside, there is no separating the world into truly independent things or beings. Thus the Buddhist statement "between principle and thing, no obstruction; between thing and thing, no obstruction" (Watts, Way of Zen, 70). So, it's only a way of speaking to say that Ed Firmage is a photographer who travels to Yellowstone and the Grand Canyon to make photographs. It's truer to say that Ed is a part of Yellowstone reflecting on itself, that he is a specimen of canny Yellowstone wildlife with an opposable digit and a taste for fine cuisine.

So, the places I visit and the photographic I (or eye) that seems separate from them are in fact inextricably interwoven. The same connection exists between me and the history of these places. The more I see of the West, learning its history as I go, the deeper this connection becomes. I can never travel along the Musselshell river without recalling John Johnston (the historical figure behind the movie Jeremiah Johnson), hike in Glacier National Park without thinking of Doug Peacock and his grizzly bears, or bounce along on jeep trails in southern Utah without saying a prayer of gratitude for the picaresque life and writings of Edward Abbey. As I drive through the colorful badlands of western Wyoming or hike in Utah's San Rafael Swell, I wonder if Butch Cassidy, the Sundance Kid, and Etta Place spread a bedroll nearby en route to Fanny Porter's Sporting House. These people and their stories have become as much a part of the landscape I inhabit as the mountains, canyons, and valleys, and like the latter have become part of me. As I go where they did, I recount, and in a small way relive, their story. My story will someday be added to theirs, and my children will travel the storied landscape to feel a connection to me.

Years before I became passionate about photographing it, I fell in love with the West. I had grown up in Utah, but, like most Utahns, seldom got out to see it. It wasn't until I was well into my thirties, on the way back from a vacation in southern California of all places, that I first experienced the magic of Utah's red rock desert. That encounter changed my life. From then on every free weekend found me hiking. Friday afternoon after work I'd head south to the desert. Saturday and Sunday I'd hike, and procrastinate as long as possible my late-night drive home and the return to work. For a year prior to taking up photography full-time, I flew to work, commuting from

Salt Lake City to San Jose every week, anticipating all the while the return to the desert. By the end of 1998, my schizophrenic existence as a weekday marketing director and weekend camera-toting hermit had become unendurable. I found myself living for the weekends and thinking that this was no way to spend the rest of my life. Time for a change.

So began my new career as a photographer, a career dedicated to the proposition that I wasn't going to spend my life "doing work I don't want to do in order to live the way I don't want to live" (thus the hero of Edward Abbey's The Fool's Progress).

My journeys around the West, like those of the mountain men and the Native Americans, tend to have a certain seasonal polarity to them. In my case, the poles are the greater Yellowstone area and northern Arizona. During a given year, I'll typically make half a dozen summer trips to Yellowstone and twice as many more during the fall and winter to the canyons of the Colorado Plateau (Capitol Reef, the San Rafael Swell, the Escalante, Bryce, Zion, Grand Canyon). But, it isn't only the big-name destinations that interest me. The entire country in between is rich in both history and scenic beauty, from the Henry's Fork River, where so much early trapping history took place, to Red Rock Junction, where a thousand feet of water from ancient Lake Bonneville broke out of the Great Basin and flowed to the Pacific, from the Wind River Mountains to Robber's Roost Canyon. The photographs in this book are a record of some of these journeys, with particular focus on five of the area's great national parks: Yellowstone, Bryce, Zion, Grand Canyon, and Painted Desert/Petrified Forest. If, as Jung suggested, my soul is embodied in my environment, then a big part of mine lies in these places. What an incarnation!

pioneer wagon, capitol reef

About the Text

Over the last couple of years I've found many companions to join Ed Abbey's ghost and me on the road. Among these are Japan's haiku poets, and it is to these unusually gifted observers of the landscape that I decided to turn for the text of Red Rock Yellow Stone.

Although people around the world have adopted it as an almost-native form of poetic expression, haiku may seem a strange accompaniment to photographs of America's western parks. In our mythology at least, the American West is a place of rugged individualists taking nature head-on with none of the refined sensibility that has given us Zen, the art of tea drinking, ethereal landscape painting on silk, and bonsai trees, in addition to haiku. Behind the bandana of our mythology, however, is a similar capability of feeling. And, behind the Japanese noh-masks, as the itinerant life of many haiku poets demonstrates, are a ruggedness and practicality that would befit a mountain man. At the level of individual experience, where haiku and photography originate, differences of national character largely disappear. East and West are more like names of the two hemispheres of the brain, which are mutually interdependent and in constant dialogue. Anima and animus, yin and yang. Any westerner can appreciate Zen, for example, because it draws on basic life experience that all of us share. I was practicing a kind of photographic Zen before I knew what to call it. Likewise, long before I came to appreciate haiku, I was making visual haiku of my own — haiku defined, in Basho's terms, as a record of what is happening here at this moment. When I did eventually encounter Zen and haiku proper, I at once sensed something familiar, but also more mature in its sensibility and formal presentation. This encounter has sparked a new internal dialogue that is evident in this book. Hopefully, the reader will find, as I do, that photography

the couch of the wild boar,
the grass lifting up —
the first dew

KYORAI

deserted by
a firefly,
the grass bending down

UTOSHI

grass, yellowstone

and haiku are mutually complementary, even ideally so, as are the experiences of photographer and poet. The haiku I have chosen and in some cases written myself are not commentaries but lyrics that give a human dimension to the song of my images. Drawing on verbal, left-brain rather than visual, right-brain skills, haiku engage parts of the mind that images can't touch. Linking haiku to my photographs is a way to involve the whole reader, or at least a wholer reader. If only books could also sing or chirp or rustle when a reader approaches! It's no accident that the oldest forms of human creativity and their contemporary descendants draw on multiple senses. Movies, for example, like ancient drama, bring together music, the spoken word (poetry in the case of drama, not prose), and visual pageantry. Perhaps in a future electronic copy of this book, you'll hear more than the rustling of these leaves as you browse its pages.

What I appreciate about haiku as a form of expression is the way it uses common experience to transcend the commonplace. At its best, it communicates in simple, brief phrases an unanticipated and powerful insight into life that commands immediate, intuitive assent from the reader or hearer. The reader is won over not by force of words or style or logic, but by the recognition of a reality already unconsciously known. The magic of haiku is to see this reality in the act of cleaning house or of picking lice from your pillow or in the sound of a door closing. Haiku is the poetry of "Aha!," of the flash of insight, not into the so-called great mysteries (about which Zen and haiku, refreshingly, have little to say) but into life. One's response is, "Yes, that's exactly the way it is." Good photography has the same effect. How often, for example, when you see an exceptional photograph of a place you've been to do you find yourself saying, "Why didn't I see that?!" This sort of response indicates that the photographer has indeed caught the essence of something, an essence that you intuitively recognize even if you've never seen the place in quite

that way. Your reaction says, "Change one detail and you diminish the whole."

By definition, the things we don't usually pay attention to — the ones considered too commonplace to matter — are the ones with the greatest potential value as revelatory catalysts. Sensitivity to ordinary little things is therefore crucial to haiku, and to all of the arts of Zen. It is no less crucial to the kind of photographs that I enjoy making. Even in extraordinary places such as the Grand Canyon or Yellowstone, the greater part of what you see is ordinary — the flowers by the wayside, the little clearings, and the common grasses, shrubs, and trees — all things that people pass and never notice in their hurry to see the grand vistas. Perhaps it's a contrarian streak of mine that delights in looking down when others are looking up, or looking at the leaves when others are gazing at the forest, but it's often these overlooked treasures that I enjoy photographing the most. It's a sensibility that I think the haiku poets shared.

roses:
the flowers are easy to paint;
the leaves are difficult

SHIKI

The fact that traffic is usually going opposite me when I head out with the camera has the huge side benefit that I can often be alone even in a park that's as crowded as a Manhattan street. I can have a private experience of a place that no one else shares except through one of my photographs. Haiku too is all about rendering a private experience. It starts with someone's being at a certain place at a certain time, and experiencing the essential quality of that conjunction of place, time, and observer. Basho, the father of haiku, defined it as "what is happening in this place at this moment."

a spring dawn:
rain falls on these trees and bushes;
no one knows it

SOJO

Unlike more lyrical appreciations of nature, such as predominate in European poetry and art, haiku is rooted in this being present. Unlike the other arts, photography too requires me to be physically present in the environment that I depict. I can't create a place through an act of pure imagination as I can with painting or storytelling.

Making a photograph is an act of creativity that links observer and observed, for, while the things depicted in the photograph exist independently of me, the ways in which they are seen to relate to one another do not. "Beauty only emerges…with the addition of a viewpoint that sees [something] as beautiful…. For this reason, patterns [substitute "photographs" or "haiku"] are not reproductions of nature, but new creations" (Yanagi, Craftsman, 113-114).

In both haiku and photography, the aha experience and the attendant moment of clarity are here and gone. It's uncanny how often the best light, at sunrise or sunset, for example, lasts just long enough to take a single photograph. A moment's inattention, and you miss your chance. As in haiku, nature reveals herself only to the attentive. This attentiveness is the real contribution of the poet or photographer. It comes in part through acute observation and in part through long acquaintance, both mediated by an openness to present experience. Thus, while the aha moments come and go, the preparation for them is a matter of the discipline of a life. Coming to understand a place like Yellowstone is not a matter of a two-day bus tour but of many returns to favorite haunts at various times of the day, in different seasons, and over many years. Coming to appreciate an area as big as that covered in this book is the task of a lifetime, a lifetime of moments of revelation.

When a haiku is successful, the poet shares the effect of seeing or realizing something in a way that transcends words. And, indeed, the form of haiku forces the poet to dispense with all but a handful of words. Comprising only 17 syllables in all (three lines of five, seven, and five syllables respectively or less commonly two lines of irregular length), haiku is, as the masters themselves recognized, a mere breath's worth of speaking. By definition, it can never be long-winded. It is thus a matter of nouns and verbs (and simple ones at that) rather than adjectives

> Since pattern is the portrayal of essence, all non-essentials must be stripped away; the pattern is what remains…'speech without words.'
>
> Pattern does not explain; it leaves things to the viewer; its beauty is determined by [the] freedom it gives to the viewer's imagination.
>
> There are many ways of seeing, but the truest and best is with the intuition, for it takes in the whole.
>
> — SOETSU YANAGI

and adverbs. The aura of things that these ancillary parts of speech would otherwise convey is left to the reader or listener to supply. The power of haiku derives from this imaginative cooperation demanded of the reader or hearer.*

The photographer faces the same challenge as the poet who must work with a limited word budget. How, for example, to capture the beauty of Grand Canyon in a piece of film that, in my case, is just 4x5 inches? How to capture the essence of a place but also only its essence. A photographer friend of mine likes to say that he seldom sees a photograph that couldn't be improved by cropping. A common mistake of the inexperienced photographer is to try to get too much in the photograph, and in so doing to lose the impact it might otherwise have. "Less is more" is not only the mantra of Zen and haiku but also of the best photographers. If haiku is arguably the strongest way of verbally conveying an experience, we could say with Edward Weston that photographic composition is the strongest way of seeing. As such, it's possible to say without arrogance that the artistic representation is more beautiful than nature. "If we see nature as beautiful, then we are, in a sense, seeing it in patterns. Pattern is the power of beauty…Pattern is the nature of nature" (Yanagi, Craftsman, 115).

---

* Note that in the English versions of Japanese haiku used here, the translators have made no attempt to retain the 5-7-5 pattern, only the essential brevity. In my own efforts, I have sometimes adhered to the 5-7-5 structure and to the other convention of classic haiku, the seasonal reference. However, the more I compare the Japanese form and its counterpart in English, the more convinced I am that the 5-7-5 structure should not be rigidly followed when a more compact expression is possible. Five syllables in English do not sound to the ear or look on the page like five syllables in Japanese, which seems much more compact both ways. Since the essence of the form is brevity, it seems counterproductive to pad a line just to make syllable count.

The experience of the natural world is central to both haiku and my kind of photography. The classic haiku anthologies are organized by season, and within each season by subjects such as sky and elements, trees and flowers, birds and insects. The great collections of Basho, Buson, Issa, and Shiki, among others, contain some of the most moving nature poetry we have in any language. Indeed, for me, it holds preeminence of place as nature writing regardless of genre (purely scientific discourse excepted). Although I share the Romantics' euphoria, I must confess that I have a hard time taking any of them (but Wordsworth in particular) seriously. The language is so overwrought, even by Victorian standards, that it becomes an impediment to the appreciation of what is, after all, a non-verbal experience — being out in nature. Haiku, by contrast, is much less dependent on formal, rhythmic, or descriptive devices that call attention to themselves as much as the great outdoors. In so far as a rendering of nature can, haiku puts you in a place and then gets out of the way so that you can enjoy it for yourself, vicariously.

Even though it deals predominantly with nature, however, haiku is not an abstract statement about nature but a means of conveying the effect of nature on a specific person, the observer. The essence of haiku is ultimately not description, nor is it poetic form, or even beauty, but the humanity of the observer in nature. It is the expression of nature in us, and of us as part of nature, "the mutual, reunited life of poet and things" (Blyth, Haiku, 4:i). Basho defined haiku as "the mind that goes off and returns." A few words about autumn leaves falling or a scene deep in the mountain sets your mind to wandering like a Romantic poet. But before you can wax too lyrical, you're brought back to concrete reality, to the suchness of a localized time and place. While reading a haiku, your mind may go off and come back more than once, but always stays connected to the ground.

The poet keeps you grounded by staying grounded himself. He does this, as the Zen monk does, by keeping a certain emotional distance between himself as observer and the experience, as also the photographer does from his subject. One way of holding experience at arm's length is to have a sense of humor about it. If you can chuckle at your situation while mosquitos and fleas are biting you, that's detachment! An example is Shiki's "autumn mosquitos / bite me / prepared to die." Issa especially seems to have liked poking fun at himself and his circumstances, not to mention the pretensions of art. While humor isn't an absolutely essential quality of photographers, it does help prevent neurosis. The photographer who can't laugh at the always-evident will of the gods to frustrate him, or who can't respond good-naturedly to the sometimes inane questions of curious bystanders will sooner or later need medical attention. One of my favorite questions is, "What are you doing?" Well, what does it look like I'm doing with this big, honkin' camera?! Another, particularly common in Yellowstone, is, "What do you see there?" My interlocutors in this case mean, "What animals do you see?" The landscape in such cases is invisible. I got this question so often I started telling people that I was photographing the rare Yellowstone spotted gnat, of which I have yet to get a really good shot. It was with a similar wink that I wrote "what do you see there? / bears hibernating, / trees busy posing." When it comes to writing haiku detachedly, my advice to myself is: if you can say something profound, great, but don't expect miracles. Since you're a product of the public schools, the odds are against you. If you can't say anything deep, at least make 'em laugh. (This too, however, is not without difficulty for a recovering Sunday School graduate). If you really feel the spirit working on you, be inspirational and funny. This is the highest art, though it continues to elude the grasp of most Americans. But the spirit of Twain works in mysterious ways.

Like today's landscape photographers, several of the great haiku poets were wanderers, traveling for years as beggars all over Japan. Their poetry is powerful because it is authentic, and it is authentic because they walked the walk of those who really know the natural world, who love it not sentimentally but in its fierceness, indifference, and even ugliness as well as its sublimity.

"traveler" shall be my name — first winter shower	the autumn wind! how many mountains, how many rivers in my heart
BASHO	KYOSHI

Being myself on the road a lot, and exposed to nature, if not red in tooth and claw, at least alternately sizzling and frigid, I'm drawn by the immediacy of the haiku poets' rendering of the world around them. And, I empathize with their alternating loneliness and love of solitude. Away from loved ones, we experience things we probably couldn't any other way. At the same time, we want to share them.

i go you stay two autumns	after the dancing the wind in the pine trees, the voices of insects
BUSON	SOGETSU-NI

Like Brother Issa, "lay priest in the religion of poetry," the landscape photographer alternately wants to get out there and be alone in some beautiful, wild place, and then to return to the comfort of a cozy restaurant or inn after a day in the cold. He needs little coaxing to bring out a Polaroid or a digital camera and show what he saw.

sensing autumn's approach four hearts draw together in a small tea room	i live with the buddha, but when it is chilly i yearn for human beings
BASHO	UNKNOWN

The photographer's is a life that unifies (or tries to) opposites: solitude and companionship, wilderness (and even wildness) and domesticity, emptiness and fullness. Ultimately, all of these experiences must bring you back into the community, reconciling the one and the many, for "apart from human beings, there is no Buddha" (Blyth, History, 2:284).

Haiku and photography are alike expressions of the ways in which our present world is being knit together. One of the hallmarks of this century has been the growing enfranchisement of people, who, in the era of the haiku masters, were often the victims of oppression. Hierarchically rigid societies based on a preferred gender, race, sexual orientation, socioeconomic background, or the like have progressively, if unevenly, given way to more inclusive ways of living together. Nowhere is this truer than in matters of soul. We are able now wherever we live to enjoy borrowed culture from around the world. Many of us are also able to experience foreign cultures at first hand. Thus, Americans have come to like sushi and haiku and the gardens of Kyoto. Thus, too, tourists from Japan have come to love hamburgers and Coke, as well as Bryce Canyon, Zion National Park, and Yellowstone. America's western parks are no longer

pioneer cabin, bear lake, id

the private reserve of a few lucky ranchers but a treasured refuge for people around the world. The intermingling of haiku and photographs from the American West is therefore representative of the cultural enfranchisement and linking of ordinary people everywhere.

One of the things that increasingly unites people is the realization that at this point we sink or swim together. A health crisis in Hong Kong can quickly become a global epidemic. Political instability in the Persian Gulf affects gas prices in Topeka, Kansas, and so on. Not all of this interdependence is good, as the many protests against NAFTA, the World Bank, the IMF, and other institutions of globalism demonstrate. With our ability to affect life globally for the worse has come the realization that we must fundamentally rethink the assumptions that have governed industrial society for the last two hundred years, assumptions that look increasingly unsustainable. Above all, people now realize that the way we treat our environment is indicative of the way we treat each other, and vice versa. There is no ultimate solution to problems in the environment that does not address issues of human rights, and no solution to the latter that ignores the effect of our actions on the environment. The industrial attitude towards nature, in which the latter is simply a resource to be used as we see fit, goes hand in hand with the abuse of people as mere functionaries in the assembly line. "What we call Man's power over Nature turns out to be a power exercised by some men over other men with Nature as its instrument" (Lewis, Abolition, 69).

under the cherry-blossoms,
none are
utter strangers

ISSA

It occurs to me, therefore, that not least among the virtues of haiku, or rather of the worldview that it represents, is the respect that it displays toward the land and the people who inhabit the land, people, who, like the poet, are intimately bound to the land. With good reason, the name of Issa, Japan's most beloved haiku poet, is paired with the epithet "gentle." To write tenderly of ordinary people and things one must respect them. It is also no accident that Zen and haiku are so often interwoven, for both celebrate the experience of receiving what ordinary life has to offer without preconditions. Both are modes of living receptively.

i believe in buddha, the green ears of the barley, the absolute truth	a man sowing barley modestly
SEISENSUI	AWAJI-JO

Walt Whitman couldn't have said it better.

Living receptively has many modes. Basic to all of them is living in a manner that is defined by the environment rather than the reverse. It means living empathetically, recognizing that the other beings around you, from frogs to redwoods, are every bit as entitled to enjoy whatever measure of happiness they can as you are. It means finding joy in the independence of these things from us, and delighting in forbearance and restraint rather than the display of our apparent superiority. This is not a sugar-coated version of the anthropic fallacy. I do not know what a tree feels, nor can I say (at least beyond the shadow of a doubt) whether elephants mourn the loss of their dead. I do know that the same force that created me also created them, and that there is therefore a priori reason to suppose that we may have some common feeling. In any event, I should mourn the loss of these beings precisely because they are different from me. So also should I mourn the loss of the landscapes these other beings call home. That form of otherness is no less a wonder for being, as we suppose, inanimate.

If humans have any particular claim to uniqueness, it is our imagination. How impoverished that and therefore we would be if the remaining wild places of the world were sacrificed to the gods of industry. How then could we sing with Ikkyu

the mind, -
what shall we call it?
it is the sound of the breeze
that blows through the pines
in the Indian ink drawing

To suppose that we could say the same thing of the breezes blowing through the strip mines of Black Mesa or the smoke stacks of the Navajo Power Plant, much less photographs of them, beggars the imagination.

Creativity, like natural fertility, comes from the wild part of life, the part that is undomesticated, instinctive, mysterious, unknown and partially unknowable, and productive of new forms. Nor is creativity simply an analogue of fertility. In fact, it draws continually and directly on wild nature for inspiration, wild not only or even primarily in the sense of wild places but of all that is fertile, ultimately beyond our ability to control, and awe-inspiring. Whether we're talking about the bucolic farm life of Virgil's Georgics, the thunderstorm of Beethoven's Pastorale, or the canyon's of Ed Abbey's solitary desert, we're celebrating things that we can at best use or imitate, never control or make for ourselves. We celebrate what is unbidden, and, in both senses of the word, free.

Edwin Firmage, Jr.
Salt Lake City, August 2004

Bibliography

- Watts, Alan. *The Way of Zen*. New York: Vintage, 1989. Originally published 1957.
- Blyth, Reginald. *Haiku*. Four volumes. Tokyo: Hokuseido, 1964-68.
- Blyth, Reginald. *A History of Haiku*. Two volumes. Tokyo: Hokuseido, 1964-68.
- Lewis, C.S. *The Abolition of Man*. New York: Macmillan, 1973. Originally published 1947.
- Yanagi, Soetsu. *The Unknown Craftsman*. Tokyo: Kodansha, 1989. Reprint of 1972 edition.

RED ROCK YELLOW STONE

journeys from yellowstone to the painted desert

above lewis canyon, yellowstone

foolish wildflower
without a trace
of bitterness

ISSA

あはう草花も苦はなかりけり

the acorns
are buried beneath
their own fallen leaves

SUIHA

團栗の己が落葉に埋れけり

tea for the fallen leaves
beer for their return

FIRMAGE

cold snap —
lilies' breath
also frozen

FIRMAGE

新涼や 豆腐驚く 唐辛

the new autumn coolness;
the bean-curd is aghast
at the red pepper

FURA

涼や
ふ驚き
唐から

isa lake, yellowstone

duck lake, yellowstone

i stopped —
the stream
flowed off alone

SEISHI

mammoth hot springs, yellowstone

nymph lake, yellowstone

upper geyser basin, yellowstone

what do you see there?
bears hibernating
trees busy posing

FIRMAGE

the voice of the pine tree —
wild
wherever it is heard

FIRMAGE

sylvan lake, yellowstone

chocolate pot geyser, yellowstone

the bright day
it is my soul, my spirit
the autumn breeze

SUIHA

norris geyser basin, yellowstone

the grasses
that have become autumn —
sitting down in them

SANTOKA

black sand basin, yellowstone

佛とも ならでうかうか 老の松

not yet having become a buddha,
the ancient pine-tree,
idly dreaming

ISSA

mammoth hot springs, yellowstone

grand canyon, yellowstone

a butterfly
left me alone
in the autumn mountains

MIDORI-JO

three times it cried,
and was heard no more,
the voice of the deer

BUSON

涼風や虚空

yellowstone river

boulder and sand bar —
all one
to the river

FIRMAGE

the cool breeze
fills the vault of heaven
with the voice of the pine tree

ONITSURA

rising
from my pine needle mat
the scent of incense

FIRMAGE

lower falls, yellowstone

金持も熊も來てのむ清水哉

millionaires
come and drink of this clear water,
and bears

SHIKI

lower slide lake at sunset

roads in the forest:
i take the one less traveled
by caterpillar

FIRMAGE

south park, jackson, wy

the stream hides itself
in the grasses
of departing autumn

SHIRAO

fall flowers,
their fading interrupted
for a group portrait

FIRMAGE

fall fungi, yellowstone

this morning
just a hoary memory,
the fog

FIRMAGE

near moulton ranch, grand teton

early autumn:
a summer shower stretches
into evening rain

TAIGI

evening drizzle
wood smoke —
an early fall

FIRMAGE

autumn winds —
look, the chestnut
never more green

BASHO

elk graze
a golden meadow,
storm clouds lowering

FIRMAGE

another year gone
hat in my hand
sandals on my feet

BASHO

since basho left us
not yet has
"the year drawn to its close"

BUSON

without you
too many and too wide
are the groves

ISSA

lovers
in a sleeping bag,
snow and leaves falling

FIRMAGE

in a short life
an hour of leisure
this autumn evening

BUSON

campfire smoke
drifts away
with my thoughts

FIRMAGE

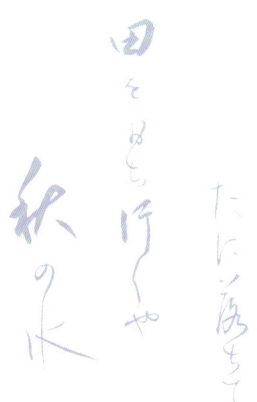

falling into the fields,
falling from the fields,
the water of autumn

BUSON

fish lake, ut

the autumn breeze
comes blowing from behind
among the grasses

SUIHA

autumn grasses, yellowstone

a hundred different gourds,
from the mind
of one vine

CHIYO-NI

boulder mountain, ut

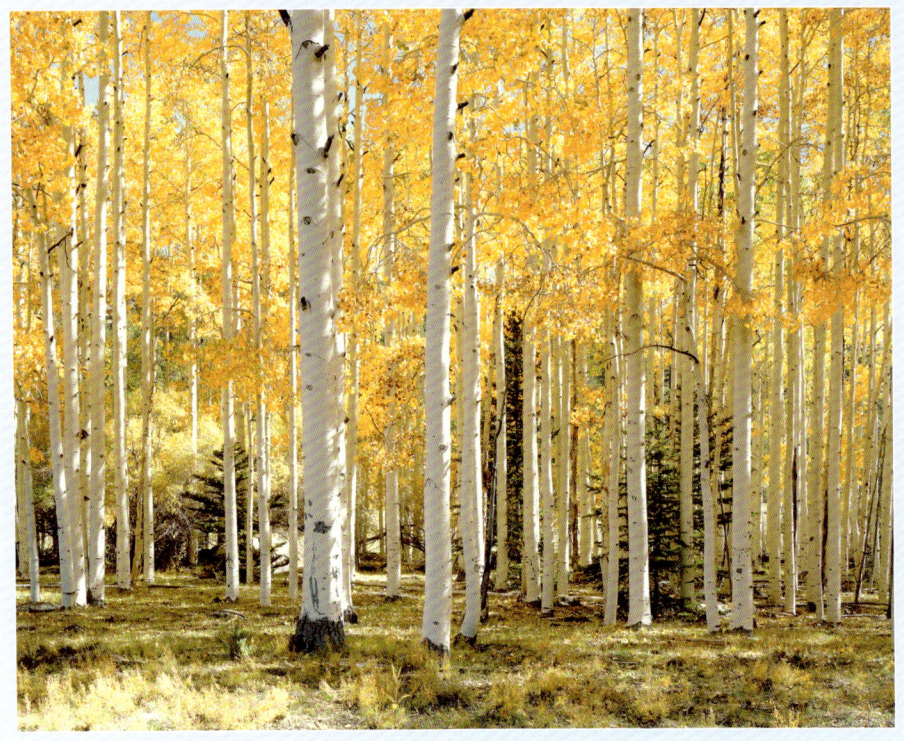

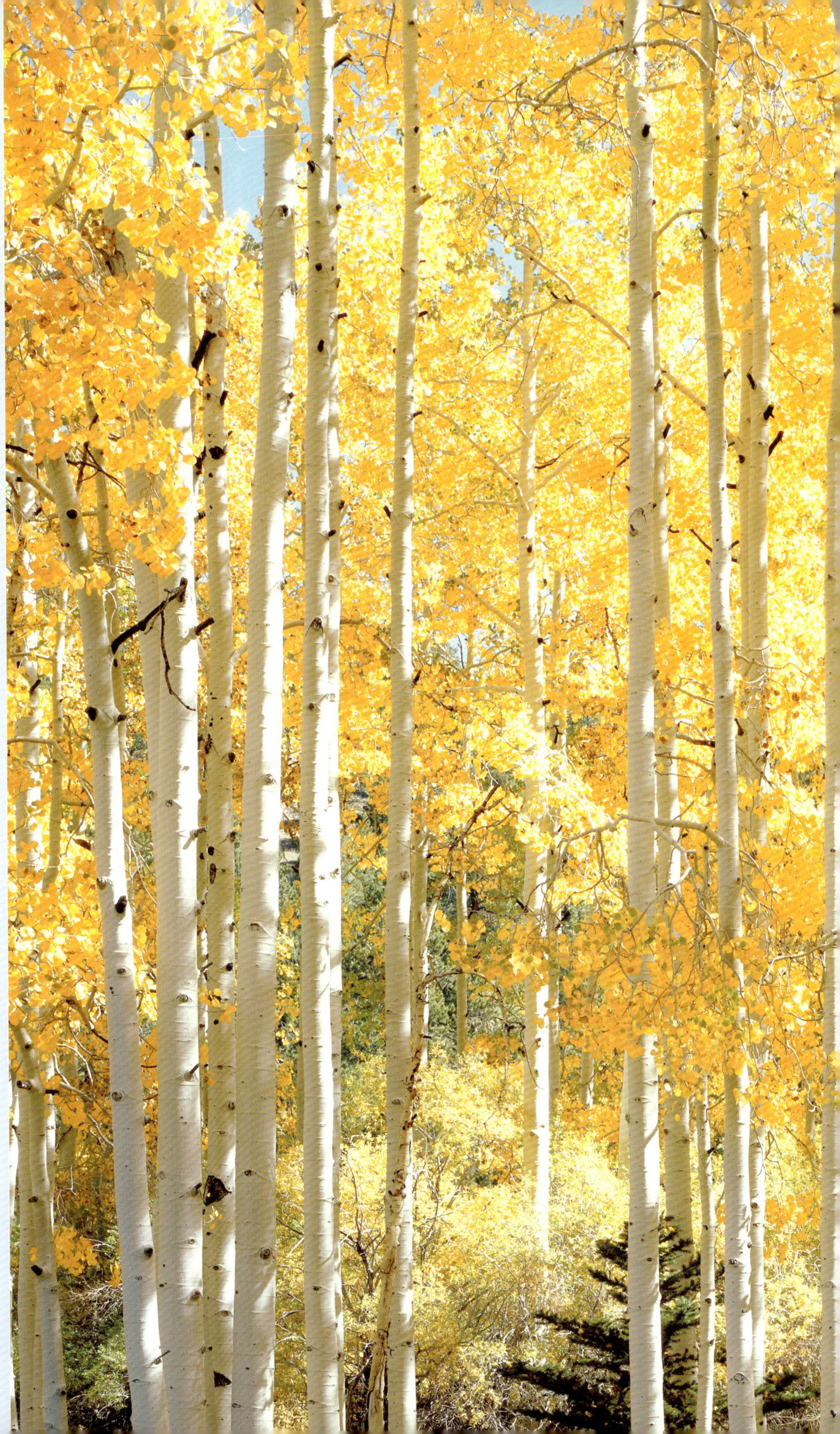

departing spring
hesitates
in the late cherry-blossoms

BUSON

like colorful birds
set free in the trees...
blossoms

ISSA

pioneer orchard —
the desert
blooming like a rose

FIRMAGE

orchard, capitol reef

良寬
木にも花
お全会

oh, cricket!
act as the grave keeper
after I'm gone

ISSA

pioneer church, near capitol reef

dry wash, san rafael swell, ut

the open road —
one bend
hidden from the next

FIRMAGE

san rafael swell

made pictures,
and footprints in the sand —
an autumn afternoon

FIRMAGE

san rafael swell

painted desert | nine mile canyon, ut

coolness —
the evening mountain
invents itself

ISSA

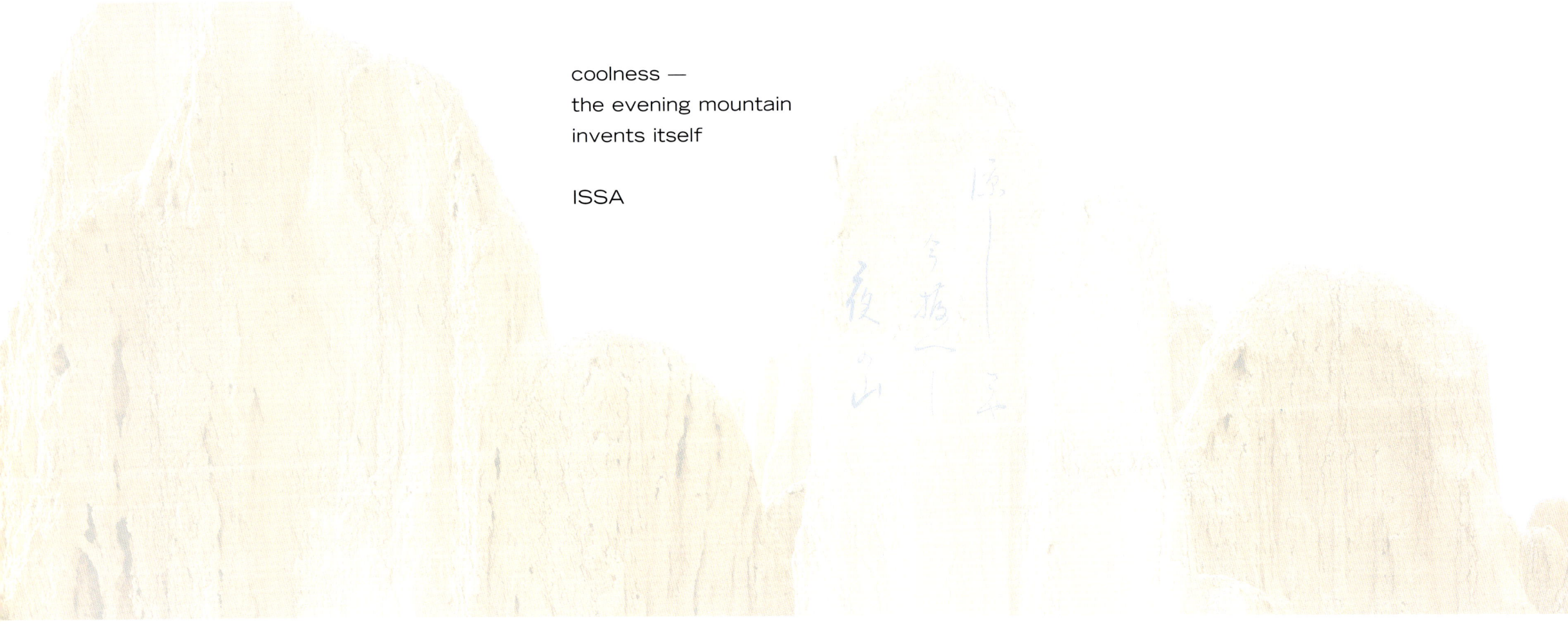

may day —
the sky too
is blooming

FIRMAGE

sunset point, bryce canyon

sunrise point, bryce canyon

the road to paradise
draws nearer...
winter cold

ISSA

bryce canyon

山鳥の尾をふむ春の入日哉

treading on the tail
of the copper pheasant
the setting sun of spring

BUSON

The voice of the fountain after midnight;
The colors of the hills at sunset

ZENRIN KUSHU

rain washed
wind polished,
not minding the season

FIRMAGE

slot canyon, san rafael swell

the names unknown
but to every weed its flower,
and loveliness

SAMPU

sitting quietly
doing nothing, the spring comes,
grass grows of itself

ZENRIN KUSHU*

narrows, zion

autumn has begun:
the sound of the wind
mingles with the river shallows

DAKOTSU

side canyon, zion

entering autumn,
the painting of flower plants
a daily task

SHIKI

under the pine trees,
autumn begins
with the stone that looks
up at the clouds

KOYO

side canyon, zion

i sit here
making the coolness
my dwelling place

BASHO

slot canyon, zion

putting the eyebrows
to the cliff, he drinks
the clear water

TOYOJO

autumn foliage on virgin river, zion

on one branch
tumbling head over heels...
autumn colors

ISSA

片枝は真さかさまに紅葉哉

taking turns
down the little waterfall…
red leaves

ISSA

north creek, zion

the subway, zion

over my legs
   stretched out at ease,
      the billowing clouds

ISSA

pioneer ruin near st. george, ut

petrified house, petrified forest

desert porcelain,
remnant of october's flood —
tea time for the flies

FIRMAGE

dried mud, buckskin gulch, ut

one of god's anointed
walking toward me
on six legs

FIRMAGE

autumn mountains
one by one
the evening falls

ISSA

point imperial, grand canyon

clear creek, zion

mixed forest, grand canyon

one more day beginning;
there are leaves
falling

HOSHA

autumn rain
last drops —
the silent grove

FIRMAGE

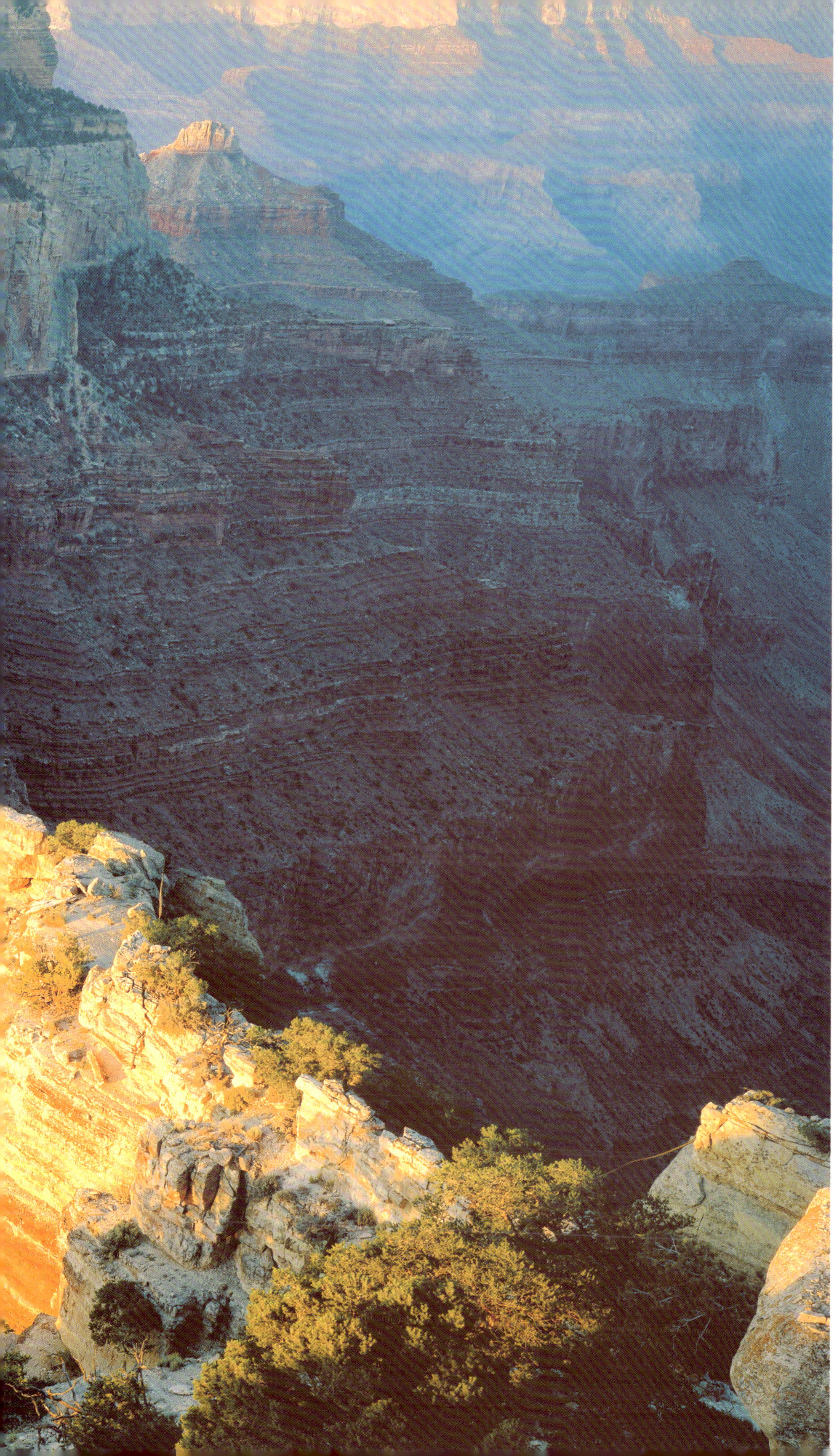

taking night
  in his arms,
    the autumn sun

FIRMAGE

not a place
to put oneself —
the heat

BOKUYA

身一つの置所なき暑さかな

petrified forest

painted desert

painted desert hills,
no place for a man to be...
unless a painter

FIRMAGE

ABOUT THE AUTHOR

A late bloomer, at least when it comes to art, I was well into my thirties before I came to appreciate photography. And, it was only after I started using the large-format camera several years later still that I began to produce prints worthy of anyone's attention.

not grown to a butterfly
this late in autumn
a caterpillar   胡蝶にも ならで秋経る 菜虫哉

BASHO

Despite the late start, I am hopeful about what lies ahead.

at autumn's end
still with hope for the future
green tangerines   行く秋の なほ頼もしや 青蜜柑

BASHO

My present work as a photographer is my third, and I suspect final, professional incarnation, though final only in the sense that I think I've found the niche where I am most happy and from which I have no particular desire to move. Hopefully it is not final in the sense that I spend more time looking backward than forward. Some time ago, the University of Utah Alumni Association asked graduates what their message for living would be and what they thought their most significant accomplishments were. Since beginning a new life for myself as a fine art photographer, my message for living comes from the fictionalized persona of Edward Abbey in his "fat masterpiece," The Fool's Progress. Abbey's alter ego says that he's tired of doing what he doesn't want to do to live the way he doesn't want to live. It was such a sentiment that prompted me to give up a high-paying career in Silicon Valley and pursue my bliss making photographs of wild places. My most significant accomplishments, I hope, are still to come — things that I will do living the life that pursuing this bliss entails.

Trained in Near Eastern Studies, I expected, in my first professional incarnation, to spend my life in a university setting teaching Semitic languages or Middle Eastern history. Instead, and altogether unexpectedly, I ended up working as a marketing director and product manager for high-tech firms in Utah and California. I won't say that I got sidetracked into marketing, because that would imply a detour from my proper path. If it weren't for my stint in marketing, I probably wouldn't have acquired the computer skills that are now essential to my work. Nor would I have gained the other kinds of expertise required to run my own business. But, more than anything, I wouldn't have had the experience of living one life from Monday through Friday, and a completely different life on the weekends. This kind of experience — of the workaday world — was a not-altogether-pleasant revelation to this cloistered academic. It helped to focus my attention on what it was that I truly wanted my life to be. Like Henry Lightcap, Abbey's fictional alter ego, I was determined after ten years of the live-to-make-money routine to spend the rest of my life doing something more fulfilling. And, for me, as for Abbey, that something was tied up with the experience of wilderness. During my marketing years, I had come to love exploring and photographing southern Utah. This weekend hobby was destined to become my third professional incarnation.

Unlike my marketing work, photography is more than a job, an identity that I put on and take off at will. It's a way of experiencing life, a discipline, visual tai chi. It is a discipline in many senses. It involves, for example, training the mind to see things that perhaps it would not otherwise be sensitive to. It also involves many other forms of technical as well as physical discipline. Photography as a form of disciplined self-expression is a way of exploring the world around me and of experiencing my connection to it. On a hot day in Zion National Park, when heat seems to penetrate my bones, it's easier to appreciate the Zen notion that, in Alan Watts' words, I am a nerve-ending through which the universe looks at itself. I understand this by leaving the city, going out into the countryside, and actively meditating through my camera.

Limited-edition Iris prints of the images in this book are available through firmageditions.

sand dunes, near st. george, ut

ACKNOWLEDGEMENTS

I'd like to acknowledge and thank the many people whose help made this book possible: the publishers and translators of the Japanese haiku, who are individually noted on the copyright page, Michio Zushi, who produced the elegant calligraphy, Shizuka Okawa, who did the word processing of the Japanese haiku, and Jim Fairchild, my design partner on this book as on its predecessor, Simple Gifts. Jim and I think a lot alike, which makes for a good partnership, but differently enough that I hear something more interesting than an echo. My father, Edwin B. Firmage, kept me financially in the game while the book was taking shape and has greatly diminished the "starving" part of "starving artist" in my case. Gary Pedroza, Craig Caviezel and Jen Schwarz through their investment made Red Rock Yellow Stone a reality. My gratitude to all three is enormous. Thanks as well to my brother, Jon, who introduced me to Gary, Craig, and Jen. As in all my work, I owe an incalculable debt to my wife, Carrol, and my children, Elizabeth, Eddie, Christopher, and Victoria, with whom travel around the West — red, yellow, and otherwise — is one of my greatest joys. The book owes much to the expert work of the talented folks at Regal Printing in Hong Kong. Lastly, I'd like to acknowledge the critical, if more general, contribution of Yellowstone National Park, its superintendents, Mike Finley and Suzanne Lewis, and Xanterra Corporation. When I was just starting out as a photographer, Mike Finley took an interest in my work and introduced me to his colleagues at Xanterra. Our first afternoon conversation about my print Yellowstone Renaissance eventually led to my now four-year-long relationship with Xanterra, a relationship that is a significant part of my business as well as the raison d'être of this book. Many people at Xanterra — executives, store managers, site managers, accountants, guides — have made my relationship with the company a pleasure, but one in particular, Jim Fowler, deserves special recognition. Jim's been an advocate and ally from day one. Ad multos annos, Jim. Needless to say, no one at YNP or Xanterra is in any way responsible for goofs, gaffes, or other forms of political or legal incorrectness that may appear here. Finally, I'd like to pay tribute to my son, Eddie, who at the ripe age of eight came up with the title for the book before I had even taken up photography full-time. Thinking of Eddie, now 14, on my most recent trip to Yellowstone, I wrote the following:

my son at fourteen,
a shoot not yet above ground —
what a blossoming!

Lake Lodge, Yellowstone, September 19, 2004

fathers and sons —
water before, water after
forever following each other

COPYRIGHT ACKNOWLEDGEMENTS

Excerpt from A. B. Guthrie, Jr., The Big Sky. Copyright © 1947, renewed 1974 by A. B. Guthrie, Jr. Reprinted by permission of Houghton Mifflin Company. All rights reserved.

Excerpts from Soetsu Yanagi, The Unknown Craftsman. A Japanese Insight into Beauty. Adapted by Bernard Leach. Tokyo: Kodansha, 1972. Reprinted by permission of Kodansha.

For the translations of Basho p. 104: Makoto Ueda, Basho and His Interpreters. Selected Hokku with Commentary. Copyright © 1992 by the Board of Trustees of the Leland Stanford Jr. University. All rights reserved. Used with the permission of Stanford University Press, www.sap.org.

For translations of the haiku on pp. 5-7, 10, 12, 13, 17, 18, 22, 31, 33, 35, 37, 39, 41, 46, 50, 52, 54, 56, 70, 73, 77, 79, 80, 82, 83, 85, 90, 99, 102: R.H. Blyth, A History of Haiku. 2 vols. Tokyo: Hokuseido, 1963 and R.H. Blyth, Haiku. 4 vols. Tokyo: Hokuseido, 1949-1952. Reprinted by permission of The Hokuseido Press.

For the translation of Basho p. 50: Lucien Stryk, On Love and Barley: Haiku of Basho. London: Penguin, 1985. Reproduced by permission of Penguin Books, Ltd.

For the translation of Seishi p. 23: Lucien Stryk, Cage of Fireflies: Modern Japanese Haiku. ISBN 0-8040-0976-7 (cloth) 0-8040-0977-5 (paper). Reprinted by permission of Swallow Press/Ohio University Press, Athens, Ohio.

For Issa p. 58: Yuzuru Miura, Classic Haiku. A Master's Selection. Boston, Massachusetts and Tokyo, Japan: Charles E. Tuttle Co. Used by permission of Charles E. Tuttle Co.

For Issa pp. 17, 56, 67, 69, 87, 88, 96: David Lanoue's web site The Haiku of Issa, http://webusers.xula.edu/dlanoue/issa/. Used by permission of David Lanoue.

For the translation of Basho p. 50 and Buson on the dedication page: The Essential Haiku: Versions of Basho, Buson and Issa. Edited with an introduction by Robert Hass. Introduction and selection copyright © 1994 by Robert Hass. Unless otherwise noted, all translations copyright © 1994 by Robert Hass. Reprinted by permission of HarperCollins Publishers, Inc.